the facts about
HABITATS

Rebecca Hunter

W

FRANKLIN WATTS
LONDON•SYDNEY

© Franklin Watts 2003

First published in 2003 by
Franklin Watts
96 Leonard Street
London
EC2A 4XD

Franklin Watts Australia
45-51 Huntley Street
Alexandria
NSW 2015

ISBN: 0-7496-4880-5

A CIP catalogue record for this book is available from
the British Library

Manufactured in China
Planning and production by Discovery Books Limited
Editor: Rebecca Hunter
Design: Keith Williams
Consultant: Jeremy Bloomfield
Illustrations: Peter Bull: page 20, page 22;
Stefan Chabluk: page 18; Stuart Lafford: page 7.

Photographs:
Bruce Coleman Collection: cover, page 4 (Gerald S Cubitt),
page 7 (Jane Burton), page 8, page 9 top, page 13 (P
Kaya), page 14 (Jeff Foott), page 19, page 23, page 21
top (Allan G Potts), page 24; Discovery Picture Library:
page 29; Oxford Scientific Films: page 5 (Alison Kuiter),
page 6 (Irvine Cushing), page 9 (Michael Fogden), page
10 (Doug Allan), page 12 top (Howard Hall), page 12
bottom (Malcolm Coe), page 15 (Kathie Atkinson), page 17
(Daniel Cox), page 18 (Brian Kenney), page 25 (Richard
Packwood), page 26 left (Keven Su), page 26 right (Peter
Weimann); Photodisc: page 11, page 27, page 28;
Science Photo Library: page 23.

the facts about

HABITATS

Contents

Words in **bold** appear in the glossary on page 30.

What is a habitat?

A habitat is the natural home of a group of plants and animals.

Habitats can be as large as a mountain or desert, or as small as a back garden pond. A habitat contains a number of **species** of plants and animals. Some habitats may have just a few plants. In the grassland habitats of South America, for example, the main plant is pampas grass. Other habitats, such as tropical rainforests, have an enormous number of plant species. Large numbers of animals live among and feed on these plants.

You can do it...

Find out about woodlice habitats. Get a large box and in the four corners put:
1. damp soil and dead wood.
2. dry sand.
3. dry leaves.
4. a pile of damp pebbles.

Now release about 6 woodlice into the middle of the box. Leave the box for an hour or so in the dark. When you go back, count how many woodlice are in each area. What does this tell you about the habitats woodlice prefer?

▼ Not many plant species can live in a desert habitat because water is so scarce. That means there are few animals either. Those animals that do live in deserts need to be able to conserve water and survive on the very limited vegetation.

▲ A coral reef is one of the richest habitats on Earth. The shallow, warm water, which is full of **nutrients**, encourages many plant and animal species to live there.

Some animals need very special food and can only live in one particular habitat. The giant panda, for example, eats almost nothing but bamboo shoots and can therefore only live in the very small areas of Chinese bamboo forest that remain.

Other animals such as red foxes and brown rats can survive in lots of different habitats. Many people living in towns and cities are familiar with urban foxes that come and raid their rubbish bins.

key facts

- A habitat is the place where plants and animals live.

- Habitats can be large or small.

- Some animals can live in only one habitat.

Communities

A community is the name given to the animals and plants that live together in a particular habitat.

In order for the community to survive and thrive, the habitat must provide it with three things. These are: food and water, shelter and a safe place to **reproduce**.

Life in an oak tree

An oak tree is a habitat for many living things. The tree, together with the animals and plants that live on and around it, make up a community.

▲ The woodpecker can often be heard drumming on a tree trunk as it searches for beetles. It is part of the tree's community.

Each part of the tree provides food and shelter for different animals. It also provides a place where other plants, such as lichens, liverworts and mosses, can grow.

Vaporer moth caterpillar

Bark beetle

Wasp

Owl

Rabbit

These are some of the animals that live in and around an oak tree.

The trunk and bark are home to a wide variety of beetles, spiders and moths. Some beetles, such as the oak bark beetle, live between the bark and the wood. You can see the pattern their tunnels make under the bark.

Oak leaves provide food for many insects. In some years a tree can have so many oak moth caterpillars that it is almost stripped of its leaves. The red oak roller, a type of weevil, uses oak leaves as a breeding ground. It rolls up a leaf and lays its egg inside the tube.

All the small animals that live on the oak tree are food for larger animals and birds. In summer, forty hectares of oak woodland can support up to 400 birds. Most of these are insect-eaters. Some birds eat the acorns produced in autumn. A wood pigeon can eat about 120 acorns a day!

Beneath an oak tree several other animals can sometimes be found. Mice and voles feed on seeds, nuts, insects and roots, while rabbits and badgers often dig their tunnels between the roots of trees. Deer are also fond of acorns, and **browse** on young shoots and leaves during the summer.

▲ The grey squirrel is commonly seen in oak trees. It feeds on shoots, nuts, berries and insects, and makes a nest of twigs and leaves high up in the tree.

key facts

- A community is all the plants and animals that live together in a habitat.

- An oak tree provides a home for many species of insects, birds and mammals.

Adaptations

To help them survive in their habitat, plants and animals have developed special features to suit the place where they live. These are called **adaptations**.

Animal adaptations

Have you ever wondered why you do not find grizzly bears in Africa or penguins in the Mediterranean Sea? Why wouldn't elephants survive on the **tundra** or flamingos in the ocean? The answer is that, over millions of years, all living species have changed and adapted so that they are able to survive well in the particular set of conditions in which they live.

▼ Wild horses are grazing animals and are adapted to living on the open grasslands. They live in herds, which gives them protection from predators.

Grazers

Gazelles in Africa, bison in North America and wild horses in Asia are all animals that are adapted to living on wide, open grasslands. They all have teeth and stomachs that are suited to **grazing** on grass, and long legs for running away from **predators**. They also live in herds, which give them protection when they have to migrate or travel long distances.

Seashore life

The limpet is adapted to living in the **tidal zone** on the seashore. When the tide is in, limpets move slowly around feeding on the small seaweeds on the rocks. When the tide goes out, the limpets clamp themselves down tightly on to the rocks so that they do not dry out. They also do this in stormy weather or if threatened by a seagull.

Camouflage

For some small animals, the biggest problem in their lives is how to avoid being eaten by predators. One way is to be coloured so they cannot be seen easily. This is called **camouflage**. For example, katydids (grasshopper-like insects whose **Latin** name means 'false leaf') look like different types of leaves.

key facts

- Plants and animals have features that allow them to live in their habitat.
- These features are called adaptations.
- Many animals have bodies that are adapted to protect them.

▼ These insects are katydids. They look very similar to the leaves among which they live.

Adapting to temperature

Animals and plants live almost everywhere on the Earth. From the freezing polar regions to the scorching **equator**, you will find living things.

Adapting to heat

The main problem that animals in hot areas have is finding ways to keep cool. They can either do this by having specially adapted bodies or by changing their behaviour.

The kangaroo rat, a rodent that lives in North and Central America, has to cope with daytime temperatures of up to 50°C. It manages to live in these hot conditions by a combination of adaptations. It spends the day asleep in a burrow and only comes out to eat at night. It does not need to drink water as it gets all the water it needs from the seeds it eats.

Camels live in not only the hottest parts of the world, but some of the driest. Their bodies are adapted to surviving on very little water. Their body temperature can rise higher than that of most other **mammals**.

▼ A camel can go without water for weeks. When it finds water it can drink up to 114 litres in one go.

Adapting to cold

The North and South poles are the coldest places on Earth. But, despite the freezing temperatures, icy waters and biting winds, many species of plants and animals live near the poles and are found nowhere else.

The huge polar bear has a thick, water-repelling fur coat that covers its entire body except for its footpads and the tip of its nose. Under the fur, it has a 10-cm layer of fat and a black skin that absorbs heat from the Sun, helping the bear warm up. Its furry-soled feet stop it slipping on the ice.

Temperate adaptations

Temperate lands often have hot summers and cold winters – a difficult climate for animals to cope with. Some animals, such as swallows, migrate to warmer lands when winter comes. Others, such as mice and bats, choose to avoid the cold temperatures by storing food as fat inside their bodies, and then sleeping, or hibernating, through the winter.

key facts

- Adaptations to temperature can be in body design or in the animal's behaviour.

- Some animals avoid extreme temperatures by migrating.

- Hibernation is an adaptation some animals have developed to avoid cold weather.

Adapting to life in water

Many animals, including fish and birds, live in water. To do this they need several special adaptations.

Fish are the animals most obviously well-adapted to life in water. Most have a **streamlined** shape which allows them to move through the water fast. They have fins to help them steer and balance, and many also have a swim **bladder**, which works like a float and allows them to change how deep they go. Fish do not need to breathe air. Instead they have **gills** that take in water and extract oxygen from it.

Penguins are birds that live in the southern oceans. They cannot fly but are excellent

▲ The sailfish is the fastest fish in the sea, and can swim at 110 kph (68 mph) over short distances. Generally, the more streamlined a fish is, the faster it swims.

swimmers, spending as much as 85 per cent of their time in the water. Using their wings as flippers, some penguins can swim faster than many fish.

Marine mammals

Many marine mammals, such as sealions, seals and porpoises, have features that are similar to fish. They have streamlined shapes, flippers that are more like fins than legs, and nostrils that close underwater. The southern elephant seal of Antarctica can dive to depths of 1,200 metres and stay under the water for nearly 2 hours.

Amphibians

Amphibians are adapted to live on land and in water. To do this they share features with both land and water animals. A frog has webbed feet and powerful legs for swimming, but it also has lungs and breathes air from above the surface. It lays its eggs in water and when they hatch the tadpoles can only survive in water.

When the tadpoles grow legs and start turning into frogs they can climb out of the water and begin their land life.

key facts

- Animals that live in water need to be streamlined.
- Fish have gills to breathe under water.
- Amphibians are adapted to live in water and on land.

Plant adaptations

Plants can also survive in most parts of the world. They have adapted to live in hot and cold areas, and also in very wet or very dry situations.

Dry conditions

The cactus family has hundreds of different species that grow in dry areas around the world. Cacti have no leaves, as these would lose water too quickly. Instead their thick, green stems do the job of **photosynthesis** (see page 16).

Cacti can take in enormous amounts of water. In **droughts**, they become shrivelled and thin. Then, when it rains, they take up water at great speed and their stems become fleshy and fat.

Thirsty desert animals are attracted to the water in the cactus stem, so the plant protects itself with sharp spines.

Cold climates

Coniferous trees are an example of plants that are adapted to living in cold, snowy conditions. Instead of delicate, thin leaves, they have needles that are covered in a tough, waxy layer, and **sap** that can survive being frozen.

▼ Cacti store water in their fleshy stems. Their roots spread out widely to collect any rain that falls.

Many conifers grow branches that slope gently downward. Snow slides off the branches rather than building up into a great weight that would break them.

Seaweeds (see right) have flexible rubbery fronds that will not be damaged by the pounding waves. They don't dry out at low tides because they are covered in a layer of **mucus**. Some seaweeds have gas-filled bladders that enable them to float on the surface of the sea and receive the sunlight they need to survive.

key facts

- Plants are adapted to live in most conditions.

- In hot areas, plants have very small leaves to avoid water loss.

- Coniferous trees have thin, waxy needles instead of leaves.

Producers and consumers

Animals and plants living together in a community are all linked together because they all depend on each other for food and nutrients.

Plant producers

Plants are called the producers in a community. This is because they produce their own food using sunlight. This process is called photosynthesis and is carried out in the leaves of plants.

Each leaf contains a green substance called **chlorophyll**. This chlorophyll can trap the energy in sunlight. The energy is used to turn water and the gas carbon dioxide into a simple sugar, called glucose. The plant then uses the glucose to grow and produce more leaves, and eventually flowers and seeds.

Plants produce an enormous amount of food for animals to eat, but that's not all. The process of photosynthesis also gives off oxygen, which is the gas that animals and people need to breathe. Plants are essential to all animal life.

► How the process of photosynthesis works.

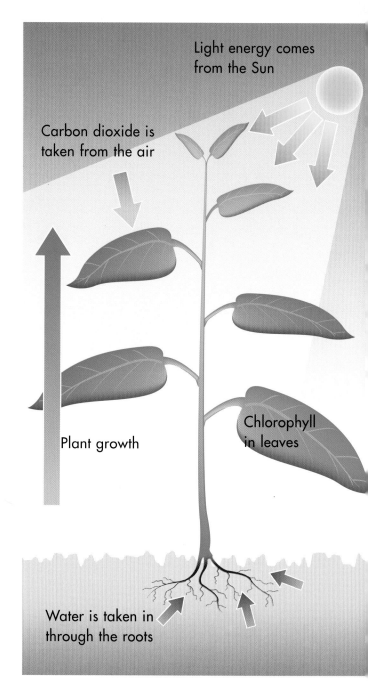

Light energy comes from the Sun

Carbon dioxide is taken from the air

Plant growth

Chlorophyll in leaves

Water is taken in through the roots

◀ Grizzly bears are carnivorous. Their sharp, pointed teeth help them catch and kill other animals.

Carnivores, or secondary consumers, are animals that live by eating other animals. Cats, dogs, wolves, tigers, crocodiles and grizzly bears are all carnivores. You can often tell if an animal is a herbivore or a carnivore by looking at its teeth. Herbivores have incisors to cut into grass and molars to grind it up. Carnivores have sharp pointed teeth for killing animals and for tearing flesh. Omnivores are animals that eat both animal and plant foods.

Consumers

Animals are consumers – they cannot make their own food. They eat plants or other animals. Herbivores, or primary consumers, are animals that only eat plants. Because plants are low in nutrients, herbivores need to spend most of their time feeding.

In the tropical savannah of East Africa about 40 species of grazing mammals share the grasslands. They are able to do this because they all feed on different parts of the grasses, shrubs and trees. Zebras, for example, eat the tops of the grass stems, while wildebeest eat the middle part and Thomson's gazelles the bottom part.

key facts

- Plants are producers – they produce their food.

- Animals are consumers – they eat plants or other animals.

- Herbivores are plant-eating animals.

- Carnivores are animals that eat other animals.

Food chains

A food chain shows how plants and animals are connected by what eats what. A food chain always starts with plants.

A plant uses the Sun's energy to grow. Plants are eaten by herbivores. Carnivores or omnivores then eat the herbivores. Sometimes another carnivore may eat the first carnivore. Animals that are eaten by others are called **prey**. Those that eat them are called predators.

Pond food chain

▶ A food chain in a pond would look like this: pond weed and algae are eaten by shrimps, snails and tadpoles; these are then eaten by small fish, newts, frogs and toads. These then become prey for larger carnivores such as bigger fish, kingfishers, foxes and otters.

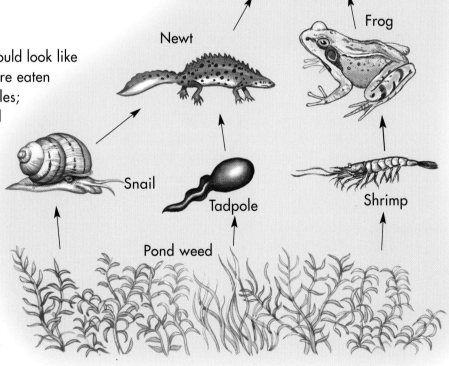

Fox (top carnivore)

Newt

Frog

Snail

Tadpole

Shrimp

Pond weed

◀ Small plant-eating animals such as this caterpillar are the second stage in the food chain.

Some animals can be part of several food chains. For example, the fox at the top of this pond food chain also feeds on rabbits, which eat grass, and mice and voles, which eat seeds and berries.

You can do it...

Draw your own food chain, with you at the top!
Think about what animals the hamburgers and fish fingers you eat come from, and what those animals might eat. You will probably find you are part of a big food chain.

▲ In an oceanic food chain, killer whales, sharks and polar bears are all top carnivores.

Top carnivores

The animal at the top of a food chain is called the top carnivore. These animals have almost no natural predators. They usually die through sickness or injury. Each continent has its own selection of top carnivores. In the Americas the top carnivores are bears, lions, eagles and alligators. In Africa there are many big cats at the top of the food chain, such as lions, cheetahs and leopards. Europe's top carnivores are bears, wolves, foxes and birds of prey.

key facts

- Food chains connect animals because of what they eat.

- Animals that eat others are called predators.

- Animals that are eaten by others are called prey.

- A top carnivore has no natural predators.

Food webs

Because most animals eat more than one type of food, they are usually part of several different food chains. These link up to make a food web.

Food webs allow energy to pass through the community. The energy comes first from the Sun. Through photosynthesis the Sun's energy is converted into plant material. When animals eat the plants, the energy moves into them and through the food web.

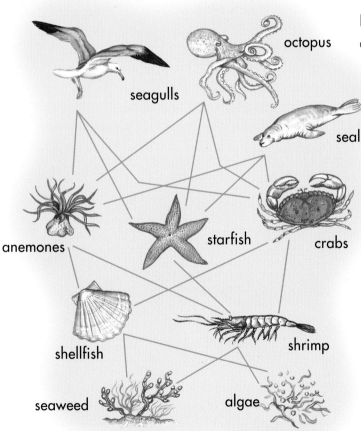

▲ Some of the plants and animals that make up a food web in a seashore habitat.

A seashore food web

A food web helps to maintain a balance in nature. If one part of a food web is altered, the rest of the web will be affected and will change accordingly.

For example, imagine that disease or pollution causes a decrease in the number of shellfish in the seashore food web. This is what would result: more seaweed, because there are fewer shellfish to eat it; fewer starfish, because they have less food; fewer crabs, not only because they have less food, but also because they will be preyed upon more often by the seagulls, who have fewer starfish to eat.

The final outcome is that the number of shellfish predators would decrease and the amount of seaweed would increase. This would provide perfect conditions for shellfish, and so eventually their numbers would increase again.

Changes to food webs

In nature this balance controls the numbers of animals quite well. But occasionally humans disrupt part of the food web in a way which causes serious change in the community.

Many birds of prey became rare in the 1960s as a result of the use of the pesticide DDT. This chemical was sprayed on crops to kill insect pests. The crops were eaten by small animals which were then eaten by birds of prey. The DDT built up in the birds' bodies and caused many of their chicks to die. The number of hawks dropped dramatically. This situation would not have sorted itself out naturally. However, since 1972, DDT has been banned in many countries and the number of birds of prey has risen again.

key facts

- Food chains combine to make a food web.

- Energy is passed around the community in a food web.

- Changing one factor in the food web causes other factors to change, too.

- Humans can affect food chains and food webs.

Decomposers

Every habitat contains organisms called **decomposers**. They are vital because they break down waste products.

In order to grow, all living things take in water, carbon, nitrogen and oxygen. These resources would soon run out if they were only used once. Animals produce waste, and eventually all plants and animals die. If there was nothing to get rid of this waste matter, it would soon make most habitats impossible to live in.

Fortunately, neither of these things happens. Both the resources and the waste matter are recycled in a process called decomposition.

Decomposers clean up the **environment** and recycle the chemicals carbon and nitrogen that are essential for the life of other plants and animals. Most of the minibeasts that live on or in the soil are decomposers. Woodlice, beetles, slugs, snails and earthworms, for example, all feed on fallen leaves and other dead plant and animal material.

Cycles in a habitat

KEY
➡ oxygen
➡ carbon/carbon dioxide
➡ nitrogen

Green plants take in carbon dioxide during photosynthesis and give out oxygen.

Animals breathe in oxygen and breathe out carbon dioxide.

Animal droppings contain carbon and nitrogen.

Carbon and nitrogen are returned to the habitat to be re-used.

Decomposers, such as worms, bacteria and fungi break down plant and animal matter.

Plants and animals die and their bodies decay.

Animals eat plants and take in carbon and nitrogen.

You can do it...

See decomposition at work by making a compost heap. Collect all the waste vegetable matter from your house, and the leaves and dead branches from your garden. Build them up in a heap. Keep the compost heap warm by covering it with a piece of old carpet or sacking, and keep it damp - decomposers like warm, wet conditions. After a few months you should find a fine compost has formed. If you spread this on your flower beds you will be giving your plants many extra nutrients.

▼ A few of the micro-organisms that live on a compost heap.

Micro-organisms

Micro-organisms are tiny living things that can only be seen under a microscope. There are two main types of micro-organism that help in decomposition: bacteria and fungi. Bacteria are the most widespread living things on Earth. They are found in the air, in the ground and all over plants and animals. Fungi are a strange group of plants; unlike green plants they cannot make their food by capturing sunlight. Fungi consist of a mass of tiny threads that live underground or in dead wood.

key facts

- Dead plants and animals are broken down by decomposers.

- Decomposers return useful nutrients to the environment.

- Micro-organisms include bacteria and fungi.

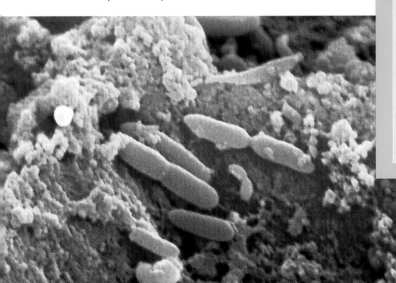

Habitats in danger

Many habitats, and the animals and plants that live in them, are in danger of being destroyed. Most damage to habitats is caused by humans.

Tropical rainforests

The tropical rainforest is the world's most diverse habitat. The forests grow in warm, wet regions near the equator. They cover less than 10 per cent of the Earth's land surface, yet over half of all the animal and plant species in the world live there.

▼ A snake in the Amazon rainforest. Tropical rainforests contain more species of plants and animals than any other habitat. That is why it is so important to protect them.

Sadly over half the rainforests on Earth have been destroyed in the last 60 years. Trees are cut down either for timber, or to clear the land for farming and building. Some forests are destroyed by mining companies looking for oil and metals. Many animals, birds and plants have already become **extinct**, and thousands more are in danger.

Temperate forests

Temperate forests that grow in parts of Europe and North America are also under threat. Many have been cut down to make way for farms and houses. Fast-growing conifers are more profitable as timber, so they are often planted instead of the natural **broadleaved** trees.

Trees are also at risk from another, chemical danger. When factories and power stations burn fuel, they release **chemicals** into the air. These mix with water in the atmosphere to make **acid** rain. Acid rain not only damages trees but eats into buildings and kills wildlife in rivers and lakes.

Polluted seas

The seas and oceans are also in danger from chemical **pollution**. Pesticides, **sewage** and chemical waste are all dumped into rivers or the sea. As a result, many seas are now seriously polluted. When oil tankers run aground, they can spill millions of litres of oil in just a few hours. This kills large numbers of fish, sea birds and animals at sea. The oil can also cover hundreds of kilometres of beaches, destroying more habitats and killing more wildlife.

▼ Sea and coastline habitats can be endangered by sewage, oil and other substances that are pumped into the water or discharged by ships.

key facts

- ○ The destruction of habitats endangers wildlife.

- ○ Tropical rainforests are the most important habitats at risk.

- ○ Pollution of the air causes acid rain.

Endangered animals

Habitats all over the world are in danger. As a result many animals are on the verge of extinction.

Giant panda

The giant panda (below) is one of the most endangered animals in the world. Its habitat, the bamboo forest of south-western China, has been greatly reduced as the forest is cut down and replaced with villages and rice fields. It is thought that there are now fewer than 400 pandas left in the wild.

▲ Golden lion tamarins are now considered a highly endangered species.

Golden lion tamarin

Golden lion tamarins are small primates that live in the coastal forests of Brazil. **Deforestation** has reduced their habitat to less than 2 per cent of what it used to be. In the small isolated areas of forest where they remain, they suffer from **inbreeding** which makes them weaker. Being small and cuddly they also suffer from another danger – being **poached** for the illegal pet trade.

Giant river otter

The giant river otter is the largest otter in the world and is found only in South America. There are less than 5,000 giant otters left and they are thought to be close to extinction. Hunting, for the otter's valuable pelt (furry skin), is the main reason, but habitat loss, pollution from mining, overfishing and diseases spread by dogs have also contributed. It is now illegal to hunt the giant river otter but poaching still happens.

Tiger

The tiger is one of the largest and most fearsome predators in the world. Tigers used to live in China, India, the Indonesian islands and as far north as eastern Russia. Now many of these populations are extinct. India has between 3,000 and 4,700 tigers, while China has less than 30 wild tigers. Loss of habitat, illegal hunting and the trade in tiger parts (which are used in traditional medicine), have all contributed to its decline.

key facts

- Many animals and plants are in danger of becoming extinct.

- The rate at which species are becoming extinct is increasing.

- Humans are destroying habitats all over the world.

Conservation

Conservation involves studying habitats, identifying the animals and plants that live there and following what happens to them.

There are many organizations that are concerned with the protection of habitats and the saving of wildlife. They include WWF, Greenpeace and Friends of the Earth.

Wildlife groups such as these are calling on governments, businesses and individual people to help with global conservation.

Some governments have responded well. For example, in Nepal the world's third highest mountain, Kanchenjunga, has been declared a special conservation area. Animals such as the red panda and the snow leopard will now be protected, as will over 25,000 species of flowering plants.

Conservation success story

The lake sturgeon is an extraordinary freshwater fish that can grow to 2.5m in length and live to be 100 years old. It was once common in the lakes and rivers of Tennessee, USA. Pollution and changes in its habitat caused the fish to die out completely in the wild. Now the river system has been cleaned up, and fish reared in captivity have been successfully re-introduced. This is part of a 25-year project to re-establish the rich **aquatic** life that once existed in this region. 1,000 lake sturgeon will be released into the river system each year for at least ten years.

◄ The endangered snow leopard is now a protected species.

Conservation begins at home

Habitats in remote parts of the world are not the only places where conservation is needed. There are plenty of habitats closer to home that need our attention. Parks, rivers, gardens and even roadside verges all provide homes for communities of animals. And all these areas can suffer from pollution and neglect.

Everyone can do their bit to preserve local habitats. Pick up litter when you see it and dispose of it properly. All rubbish is dangerous to animals: plastic bags can suffocate them, broken glass will cut their feet and metal ringpulls from cans can be swallowed by grazing animals such as cows and sheep.

▶ Everyone can do their bit for conservation. Recycling bottles and cans is one way in which everyone can help the environment. Both glass and cans are dangerous to wildlife if they are disposed of carelessly. Recycling products also means that fewer natural resources are used up in making things.

key facts

- Conservation is the studying and preserving of wildlife.

- Wildlife groups and governments are working together to save endangered species and their habitats.

- Everyone can do something to reduce pollution and conserve wildlife species.

Glossary

Acid A chemical substance that can dissolve, or wear away, other materials.

Adaptation The way in which animals and plants change over many generations to survive better in their particular environment.

Aquatic Something that lives or grows in or near water.

Bladder A bag-like part of a plant or animal that can be filled with water or air.

Broadleaved A tree such as an oak or beech that has broad, flat leaves.

Browse To eat the leaves on bushes and trees.

Camouflage A colouring or pattern that an animal has to help it hide in its surroundings.

Carnivore An animal that lives on a diet of meat.

Chemicals Substances that can be mixed together to make useful products. Used in agriculture, food manufacture and industry.

Chlorophyll The green pigment in plants that is used in photosynthesis.

Decomposer A tiny organism that breaks down dead matter. Bacteria and fungi are both decomposers.

Deforestation The removal of trees from an area.

Drought A long period with no rain.

Environment The area that makes up the surroundings of an animal or plant.

Equator The imaginary line around the centre of the Earth.

Extinct When all members of a species of plant or animal have died out.

Gills The organs in fish that allow them to breathe underwater.

Graze To eat grass.

Herbivore An animal that eats only vegetable matter.

Inbreeding When animals breed with their close relations. This results in weak or deformed young.

Latin Language used by the ancient Romans.

Mammal Warm-blooded animal that has fur and that feeds its babies on milk.

Mucus A slimy substance that plants and animals produce.

Nutrients The parts of food which the body needs for energy or to build new cells.

Omnivore An animal that eats both plants and meat.

Photosynthesis The method by which plants make food from sunlight, water and carbon dioxide.

Poaching To hunt and kill animals illegally.

Pollution When the land, water or air around us have been made dirty.

Predators An animal that hunts and kills other animals for food.

Prey Animals that are hunted by other animals and killed for food.

Reproduce When animals and plants produce more of their own kind.

Sap The liquid that flows through a plant, carrying food and water.

Sewage The waste that is collected from household toilets and drains.

Species A group of plants or animals that look alike and can breed with each other successfully.

Streamlined Having a smooth, slim shape that will move easily through water or air.

Temperate Describing an area that has a climate with mild summers and cool winters.

Tidal zone The area on the beach that is exposed between high tide and low tide.

Tundra Cold, treeless plains in the northern hemisphere near the Arctic Circle.

Further information

Books

All Kinds of Animals (It's Science)
Sally Hewitt,
Franklin Watts, 1998

All Kinds of Habitats (It's Science)
Sally Hewitt,
Franklin Watts, 1998

Food Chains (Straightforward Science)
Peter Riley,
Franklin Watts, 1998

Websites

Tiger Foundation
An organization working to ensure that tigers and their habitats are protected in Asia.
http://www.tigerfdn.com/

Office of Naval Research: Oceanography
This site is packed with waves of information on ocean water, habitats, regions, salty experiments, and more. There are some interesting naval discoveries too, so dive in!
http://www.onr.navy.mil/focus/ocean

Dian Fossey Gorilla Fund
An organization dedicated to the conservation and protection of the mountain gorilla and its habitat in Africa. Includes facts about gorillas and a biography of conservationist Dian Fossey.
http://www.gorillafund.org/

Rainforest Alliance
Dedicated to saving the rain forests. Learn about this valuable, vanishing habitat.
http://www.rainforest-alliance.org/

Polar Bears International
Working to preserve the polar bear and its habitat.
http://www.polarbearsalive.org/

Wild Lives: Elephant
Get a quick fact file, picture and information about this animal's physical characteristics, habitat, behaviour, predators and more. Includes little-known facts from the African Wildlife Foundation.
http://www.awf.org/wildlives/71

Greenscreen
Articles written by kids for kids on science and the environment. The Global Habitat Project promotes environmental awareness for young people.
http://www.greenscreen.org

Places to Visit

UK
The Natural History Museum
Cromwell Road, London SW7 5BD

Oxford Museum of Natural History
Parks Road, Oxford OX1 3PW

Royal Museum
Chambers Street, Edinburgh EH1 1JF

Royal Botanic Gardens
Kew, Richmond, Surrey TW9 3AB

Australia
Australian Museum
6 College Street, Sydney NSW 2010

New Zealand
Canterbury Museum
Christchurch Botanic Gardens, Christchurch

Index